UML
Pocket Reference

UML
Pocket Reference

Dan Pilone

O'REILLY®

Beijing · Cambridge · Farnham · Köln · Paris · Sebastopol · Taipei · Tokyo

UML Pocket Reference
by Dan Pilone

Copyright © 2003 O'Reilly & Associates, Inc. All rights reserved.
Printed in the United States of America.

Published by O'Reilly & Associates, Inc., 1005 Gravenstein Highway North,
Sebastopol, CA 95472.

O'Reilly & Associates books may be purchased for educational,
business, or sales promotional use. Online editions are also available
for most titles (*safari.oreilly.com*). For more information, contact our
corporate/institutional sales department: (800) 998-9938 or
corporate@oreilly.com.

Editor:	Jonathan Gennick
Production Editor:	Brian Sawyer
Cover Designer:	Emma Colby
Interior Designer:	David Futato

Printing History:

June 2003:	First Edition.

0-596-00497-4
[C]

Contents

UML Pocket Reference

Introduction

Welcome to the *UML Pocket Reference*. This book is written for an audience familiar with object-oriented programming (OOP) and the Unified Modeling Language (UML). It is not intended to teach UML from the ground up. Rather, it provides a convenient reference for those times you know there is a way to do something but are unsure of the syntax. This book covers UML 1.4, as defined by the Object Management Group (OMG).

UML provides a common, simple, graphical representation of software design and implementation. It allows developers, architects, and experienced users to discuss the inner workings of software. UML can express detailed design at the class level, show where concurrency and parallelism can be used to increase performance or robustness, and capture how a system must be configured and installed.

There's some tension over how best to refer to UML; some authors prefer "the UML," while others prefer simply "UML." Though strictly speaking "the UML" is grammatically correct, this book uses the more colloquial "UML."

Whenever it is useful to help clarify UML syntax or semantics, this book uses a comparison to a concrete language mapping in Java™ or C++.

Typographic Conventions

The following typographic conventions are used in this book:

`Constant width`
> Used in UML syntax diagrams. Also used in text to refer to class names, stereotype names, and other text taken from diagrams in this book.

`Constant width italic`
> Used in UML syntax diagrams to indicate user-supplied elements.

`[Optional element]`
> Square brackets surround syntax elements that are optional.

Italic
> Used to introduce new terms and indicate URLs and filenames.

...
> Ellipses indicate where nonessential material has been omitted for clarity in an example.

Note that UML makes frequent use of curly braces ({}) and guillemots («»). When used in a syntax definition, they are required by UML.

Acknowledgments

This book would not have been possible without the support of several people. First, I'd like to thank my editor, Jonathan Gennick, for his hard work and excellent advice while trading draft copies of this pocket reference with me.

Next, I'd like to thank the technical reviewers, Donald Bales and David Thomson. Their experience and knowledge helped make this book what it is.

Finally, I'd like to thank my wife, Tracey, for her support and "gentle" encouragement and my newborn son Vincent for helping me get use out of those hours between midnight and 2 A.M.

Static Modeling with UML

Static modeling captures the fixed, code-level relationships contained within a system. Static modeling encompasses the following diagram types:

- Class diagrams
- Object diagrams
- Component diagrams
- Deployment diagrams

Static modeling, by definition, does not include dynamic specifications, such as concurrency (see "Activity Diagrams"), state transitions (see "Statechart Diagrams"), or object lifetimes and communication (see "Sequence and Collaboration Diagrams").

UML Classifiers

Static modeling makes heavy use of UML classifiers. The following types of UML classifiers are used to show the structural and behavioral layout of a system:

Class
A class describes a name, attributes, operations, and responsibilities that are shared by multiple objects. Classes are blueprints for runtime objects.

Component
A physical piece of a system that realizes one or more interfaces. A component is similar to a subsystem; however, it is typically smaller and contained within a more encompassing subsystem.

Datatype
A fundamental type, typically built into an implementation language. For example, C++ supports `int`, `double`, `char`, and so forth.

Interface
An interface provides operation signatures but no implementations. An interface is typically used to define a service that one or more classes implement or realize (see "Realization" in "Classifier Relationships" for more information).

Node
A physical installation of the system at runtime. Nodes are used in deployment diagrams to show how various pieces of the system relate at a higher level than classes, components, or even subsystems. A node is typically used to represent distinct pieces of the system that may reside on one or more computers.

Signal
A signal represents an asynchronous call between two instances of a class. Signals are commonly used in message-passing systems to show the various messages.

Subsystem
Similar to a component, a subsystem provides a realization of one or more interfaces. A subsystem is almost always made up of multiple classes and often contains multiple components.

Use case
A collection of requirements for a system, described as a sequence of interactions with the user. A single system has many use cases, each providing some measurable piece of functionality when invoked by the user.

Stereotypes

All static UML diagrams share several UML elements and extension mechanisms. One such mechanism is UML *stereotypes*. Stereotypes provide a way of extending UML by defining simple terms and using them to clarify UML elements and their participation in a system. Stereotypes are typically one word, such as interface, exception, import, or library. The complete list of predefined stereotypes is at the end of this section. Stereotypes are displayed between « and » near or within the stereotyped element. For example, in Figure 1 ChecksumValidator is marked as a utility class, while InvalidChecksumException is identified as an exception.

Figure 1. A simple class diagram showing stereotypes

Rather than show stereotypes in the textual form, UML allows you to define an icon that may be used to represent a stereotype graphically. For example, the stick-and-lollipop representation of interfaces described in the "Class Diagrams" section is a graphical, iconic representation of the interface stereotype.

Stereotypes apply to nearly all of UML, though some stereotypes make sense only when attached to the correct type of element. The following list shows the predefined UML stereotypes and the UML elements to which they may apply. You can define additional stereotypes as needed.

Actor
> Applies to a class. Represents a specific role related to performing a use case.

Access
> Applies to a dependency. Shows that the originating package uses the public elements of the ending package.

Association
> Applies to the end of a link. Shows that the ending object has an associative relationship with the object at the other end of the link.

Become

Applies to a message. Shows that the ending object is the same as the sender of the message, though it may have changed values or state.

Bind

Applies to a dependency. Shows that the originating class instantiates the ending template with the specified template parameters.

Call

Applies to a dependency. Shows that the originating operation calls the ending operation.

Copy

Applies to a message. Shows that the target element is an exact copy of the source element.

Create

Applies to an event or message. Shows that the ending element is created by the source element.

Derive

Applies to a dependency. Shows that the originating element can be derived from the ending element.

Destroy

Applies to an event or message. Shows that the ending element is destroyed as a result of the event or message.

Document

Applies to a component. Shows that the given component is a document.

Enumeration

Applies to a class. Shows that the class is an enumeration.

Exception

Applies to a class. Shows that the class is an exception.

Executable

Applies to a component. Shows that the component can be executed.

Extend
> Applies to a dependency. Shows that the originating use case extends the ending use case.

Facade
> Applies to a package. Shows that the stereotyped package is really a controlled view into another package.

File
> Applies to a component. Shows that the stereotyped component is a file containing code or data.

Framework
> Applies to a package. Shows that the stereotyped package contains implementations of design or architectural patterns.

Friend
> Applies to a dependency. Shows that the originating element is not bound by the usual visibility constraints of the ending element.

Global
> Applies to the end of a link. Shows that the ending element is visible in the global scope.

Import
> Applies to a dependency. Shows that the public elements of the ending package are imported into the namespace of the originating package.

Implementation
> Applies to a generalization. Shows that the descendant class inherits its parent's implementation but does not honor the substitution principle and cannot be used as a replacement for its superclass.

ImplementationClass
> Applies to a class. Shows that the stereotyped class is an implementation in a specific programming language.

Include

Applies to a dependency. Shows that the originating use case incorporates the behavior of the ending use case.

InstanceOf

Applies to a dependency. Shows that the originating object is an instance of the ending class.

Instantiate

Applies to a dependency. Shows that the originating class creates objects of the ending class.

Interface

Applies to a class. Shows that the operations on the stereotyped class define a service the class represents.

Invariant

Applies to a constraint. Shows that the constraint must always be true.

Library

Applies to a component. Shows that the stereotyped component is a static or dynamic library.

Local

Applies to the end of a link. Shows that the ending object is in the local scope.

Metaclass

Applies to a UML classifier. Shows that a classifier's instances (objects) are classes.

Model

Applies to a package. Shows that the package is a self-contained representation of a system.

Parameter

Applies to the end of a link. Shows that the object is a parameter.

Postcondition

Applies to a constraint. Shows that the constraint must be true after the execution of an operation.

Powertype

Applies to a class or dependency. Shows a classifier whose instances (objects) are children of the given parent.

Precondition

Applies to a constraint. Shows that the constraint must be true before executing an operation.

Process

Applies to a class. Shows a classifier whose instances are full operating-system processes.

Refine

Applies to a dependency. Shows that the originating element is a further refinement (less abstract) than the ending element.

Requirement

Applies to a comment or note. Shows that the comment or note represents a requirement of a system.

Responsibility

Applies to a comment. Shows that the comment represents a responsibility of an associated class.

Self

Applies to the end of a link. Shows that the ending object is the same object as the source message.

Send

Applies to a dependency. Shows that the originating operation sends the ending event.

Signal

Applies to a class. Shows that a class represents an asynchronous piece of information exchanged between objects.

Stereotype

Applies to a class. Shows that the class is actually a stereotype that can be applied to other elements.

Stub

 Applies to a package. Shows that the stereotyped package acts as a fake (stubbed) version of another package.

Subsystem

 Applies to a package. Shows that the stereotyped package contains a group of related functionality, which can be implemented with other, unexposed elements.

System

 Applies to a package. Shows that the stereotyped package contains a complete system.

Table

 Applies to a component. Shows that the stereotyped component represents a database table.

Thread

 Applies to a class. Shows that instances of the class are lightweight operating-system threads.

Trace

 Applies to a dependency. Shows that the originating element is an earlier (in execution time) version of the ending element.

Type

 Applies to a class. Shows that the class represents the structure and responsibilities of an object but not its implementation. Similar to an abstract class.

Use

 Applies to a dependency. Shows that the originating element uses the ending element's public interface.

Utility

 Applies to a class. Shows that the class's attributes and operations are of classifier scope (static). Typically, such a class is not instantiated.

Notes

All diagrams support the use of UML notes. Notes are simply text added by the modeler to include outside information not captured in UML. For example, the modeler may use notes to present questions or comments to the developers, provide a URL to a detailed requirements document, or introduce a snippet of pseudocode to help explain some relationship.

Notes are represented as dog-eared rectangles, as shown in Figure 2.

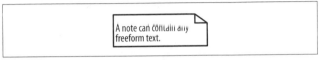

Figure 2. A UML note

Notes can be placed anywhere on a diagram and can be connected to one or more UML elements using the *note anchor line*, as shown in Figure 3.

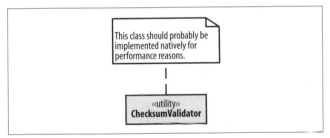

Figure 3. An anchored note

UML predefines the requirements stereotype for use with notes. Unsurprisingly, this stereotype is used to show that a given note contains system requirements.

Tagged Values

UML elements support the use of tagged values to specify user-defined properties for an element. These properties apply to the element itself and typically contain metadata external to the runtime information of a system, such as information used by a packager or the execution environment. Common uses for tagged values include conveying author-name, version, or dependency information. Figure 4 shows author and version tags on a simple class.

Figure 4. A class with tagged values

The tagged-value syntax is simply:

```
{ [tag =] value }
```

This syntax includes the following user-defined elements:

tag
> A short textual name of the property. As shown in the syntax, this is optional if the property to which the value applies is unambiguous. However, I highly recommended that you use tags to avoid possible confusion.

value
> The actual value of the property. The type and syntax of the value depends on the property.

UML predefines the following four properties, but you can add more as needed:

documentation
> Usable on any element, this property contains the documentation for the element. Some tools support this property but show the information in another compartment or window, or only in generated code.

---

location
> This property applies to most elements and identifies where an element executes. The value of this property typically references a node or component defined in a system. (See "Deployment Diagrams" for more information.)

persistence
> This property applies to classes, associations, and attributes (see "Class Diagrams" for more information). Persistence refers to whether an element's value is saved when a system is restarted. The suggested values are persistent and transient.

semantics
> This property applies to classes and operations and is similar to documentation (see "Class Diagrams" for more information). The value of this property details the element and its intent.

Constraints

Relationships between elements, as well as the elements themselves, can be validated using constraints. Constraints allow you to express conditions that must be true for the model to be valid. Like tagged values, constraints are specified between braces and are textual representations of a condition. Constraints have the following syntax:

    { textual constraint }

The textual constraint may consist of simple expressions, full sentences, or formal constraint syntax. UML defines a formal grammar, named the *Object Constraint Language* (OCL). The OCL is described in *The Unified Modeling Language Reference Manual* (Addison Wesley) and in *UML in a Nutshell* (O'Reilly).

Constraints can be placed near the constrained element or linked between relationships by using a dashed line, as shown in Figure 5.

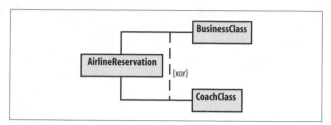

Figure 5. An example constraint

Alternatively, UML allows constraints to be placed in notes and attached to the associated element.

UML defines the following constraints, though the modeler can add more as needed:

Complete
> Applies to a generalization. Shows that the subclasses of the element are the final descendants of the superclass.

Destroyed
> Applies to an instance or end of a link. Shows that the instance or link is destroyed upon completion of the operation.

Disjoint
> Applies to a generalization. Indicates that an instance of the superclass cannot be an instance of more than one of its subclasses. This is the default reading of a generalization.

Implicit
> Applies to an association. Specifies that the relationship does not physically exist but is implied semantically.

Incomplete
> Applies to a generalization. Shows that not all the subclasses have been shown and that other subclasses are permitted.

New
> Applies to an instance or link. Shows that the instance or link is created as a result of the operation.

Overlapping
> Applies to a generalization. Indicates that an instance of the superclass can be an instance of more than one of its subclasses. However, this constraint does not guarantee that will happen; it merely allows it to happen.

Transient
> Applies to an instance or link. Shows that the instance or link is created during the execution of an operation but is destroyed before the operation completes.

Xor
> Applies to multiple associations. Shows that for the constrained associations, only one association actually exists for a given object.

Class Diagrams

Class diagrams are used to model the static relationships between components of a system. A single UML model can have many class diagrams, showing the same system from different views. For example, a class diagram may show several classes using a subsystem interface but not elaborate on the details of the implementation of the subsystem. A different class diagram, one used by the subsystem developers, may show both the subsystem interface and the classes that help realize that subsystem.

Figure 6 shows a sample class diagram.

Classes

Classes represent concepts within a system. They are typically named using nouns. A single class represents one or more objects in the system at runtime. (Class multiplicity is explained in more detail later in this section.)

Each class is made up of multiple compartments. Compartments can be named or anonymous. In its simplest form, a class has just one anonymous compartment showing the class's name. A more typical representation consists of three

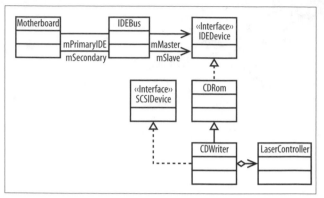

Figure 6. A sample class diagram

compartments: one showing the class's name, one showing its attributes, and one showing its operations (see "Attributes" and "Operations"). Additional compartments can be added when needed—for example, to show responsibilities, exceptions, or mutexes. However, *The Unified Modeling Language User Guide* (Addison Wesley) recommends using them sparingly to avoid cluttering diagrams. Figure 7 shows several compartments in a class.

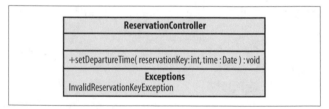

Figure 7. Anonymous and named compartments

Classes can appear on multiple class diagrams and need not show all their detail on every diagram. It is a common practice to hide (or *elide*) operations and attributes that are not relevant to a given diagram. Such omitted operations and attributes are often indicated by an ellipsis (...), as shown in Figure 8.

Figure 8. A sample class with elided attributes and operations

Class names, pathnames, and scope

Class names are usually made up of letters and can also include numbers. Though a name can be arbitrarily long and include punctuation, using any punctuation other than underscores is unusual. Colons are not permitted, as they are used to divide the components of the full pathname of the class.

Pathnames are used to represent scope, as each class within the same scope must be named uniquely. For example, the following fully qualified names refer to different classes:

```
com::oreilly::editor::SpellChecker
org::openoffice::editor::SpellChecker
```

The names before SpellChecker refer to the containing packages (see "Packages").

Multiplicity

Like many other components of UML, the multiplicity of a class can be specified by placing a number in the upper-right corner of the topmost compartment, as shown in Figure 9.

Figure 9. Class multiplicity (showing a singleton)

Classes differ from typical UML multiplicity; without a multiplicity specifier, classes default to more than one allowable instance. For example, as shown earlier in Figure 6, the Motherboard class can be instantiated multiple times. However, by specifying a multiplicity of 1, Figure 9 conveys that the class should be a singleton. It is not uncommon to see a singleton class stereotyped with <<singleton>>. However, this stereotype is not officially part of UML.

Attributes

Attributes of a class are shown in the second compartment, as shown in Figure 10.

```
┌─────────────────────────────┐
│      Motherboard        ¹    │
├─────────────────────────────┤
│ - mPrimaryIDE : IDEBus       │
├─────────────────────────────┤
│ ...                          │
└─────────────────────────────┘
```

Figure 10. Example attributes

An attribute is written as follows:

```
[visibility] attributeName [multiplicity]
[: attributeType] [= defaultValue]
[{property}]
```

This syntax contains the following user-defined elements:

visibility
    Shown as +, #, or -, for *public, protected*, or *private*, respectively. To accommodate Java's default (*package-protected*) visibility, some tools have introduced ~, though this is not strictly part of the UML specification. If no visibility specifier is used, the attribute is public by default.

multiplicity
    Used to indicate the multiplicity of the attribute. Typically, the attribute is represented as an array or vector, depending on the language. The multiplicity is expressed in standard UML notation (e.g., [0..2], [1..*], [3], etc.). If not specified, the default multiplicity is 1.

attributeType
> The type of the attribute. Typically, the attribute type is the name of another class or a basic type, such as integer or string.

property
> Shows the mutability of the attribute. Must be one of the following values:

Changeable
> Indicates there are no restrictions on the attribute. This is the default.

AddOnly
> Specifies that once a value has been added to the attribute, it cannot be removed. Applies to attributes with a multiplicity greater than 1.

Frozen
> Indicates that the attribute's values cannot be changed once they are set. This typically maps to const or final, depending on the target language.

In addition to being shown within a class, attributes can be represented as role names on relationship lines between classes (see "Classifier Relationships").

Attributes can be specific to an instance or object of a class, in which case an attribute is considered to be of *instance scope*. Attributes can also be shared between classes (static in C++ or Java), in which case an attribute is considered to be of *classifier scope*. Attributes with classifier scope are underlined in the class, as shown in Figure 11.

Figure 11. A classifier (static) attribute

Operations

Operations are typically represented in the third compartment of a class, as shown in Figure 12.

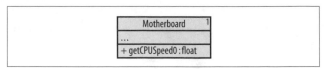

Figure 12. An example operation

Like attributes, operations can be elided (...) when they are not relevant to the current diagram. An operation is defined as follows:

```
[visibility] operationName
[(parameterList)] [: returnType]
[{property}]
```

This syntax includes the following user-defined values:

visibility

Shown as +, #, or -, for *public*, *protected*, or *private*, respectively. To accommodate Java's default (*package-protected*) visibility, some tools have introduced ~, though this is not strictly part of the UML specification. If the visibility of an operation is not shown, the operation is public by default.

parameterList

Shows the arguments to the operation. If there is more than one parameter, simply separate parameters with a comma. The syntax for parameters is as follows:

```
([direction] parameterName
: parameterType [= defaultValue])
```

This syntax contains the following user-defined values:

direction

Indicates whether the parameter is an input value (unmodifiable), an output value, or both. Must be one of in, out, or inout.

parameterName
> A valid UML name.

parameterType
> Indicates the type of the parameter. Typically, the parameter type is a class name or a basic type, such as integer or string.

defaultValue
> The initial value of the parameter if a value is not specified by the caller.

returnType
> The return type of the operation. Typically, the return type is a class name or a basic type, such as integer or string.

property
> Provides additional information about an operation. The property must be one of leaf, isQuery, sequential, guarded, or concurrent. See "Properties of operations."

Polymorphism

UML makes a distinction between an operation and a method. An *operation* is a signature that defines the operation name, its arguments, and its return type. A *method*, on the other hand, is an implementation of an operation. Multiple classes in an inheritance hierarchy can have the same operation. For example, they may each define an edit operation, but each class may define its own implementation of that operation.

Operations are polymorphic by default. This means that subclasses (classes further down the inheritance hierarchy) can provide their own implementation of an operation, rather than inheriting their parent's method. However, the leaf property is used to state that the given operation cannot be overridden by subclasses. The leaf property is mapped to final in Java and non-virtual in C++.

Properties of operations

As the syntax for operations shows, you can associate a property with each operation. The following properties are valid:

isQuery
> Indicates that an operation will return a value without modifying the class in any way. This property can be mapped to a const method in C++.

sequential
> Indicates that an operation must be called in only one thread of execution at a time. In other words, the operation is not thread safe, and the caller must control access properly. The behavior of a sequential operation is considered undefined if multiple threads use it at a single time.

guarded
> Similar to sequential, but the operation itself enforces the rule that only a single thread can call the method at any given time. Concurrent calls to this operation are handled sequentially by the operation, without effort on the part of the caller. This property can be mapped to a synchronized method in Java.

concurrent
> Indicates that an operation is guaranteed to be thread safe and can handle multiple concurrent callers.

Abstract operations

Unlike attributes, operations can be abstract, meaning the class provides no implementation. Abstract-operation names are shown in italics. This typically indicates that the owning class is an abstract class, and its name is shown in italics as well. Figure 13 shows an example of an abstract operation. The implementation for such an operation must be provided by a subclass.

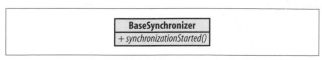

Figure 13. An abstract operation

Operation scope

Operations can be scoped to the instance of the class, in which case they are considered to be of *instance scope*. Operations can also be shared between objects (static), in which case they are considered to be of *classifier scope* and are underlined, as shown in Figure 14.

Figure 14. An operation of classifier scope

Template classes

Several programming languages allow a developer to design a class without specifying the exact types on which the class operates. At a later time, the user of a template class can specify the target types and retain type safety during compiles. UML allows modeling of template classes by simply overlaying a dotted box that contains the template parameters in the upper-right corner of a regular class, as shown in Figure 15.

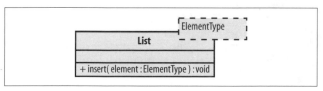

Figure 15. A template class

Associating a real type with a template class is called *binding*. UML provides two ways of representing template binding. The first is similar to the C++ syntax for templates, in which you simply define a class named with the template arguments. This is called *implicit binding* and is shown in Figure 16.

Figure 16. Implicit binding

The alternative to implicit binding is *explicit binding*, represented using a stereotyped dependency relationship, as shown in Figure 17.

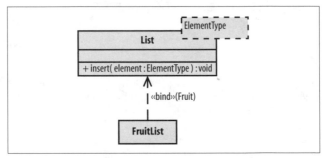

Figure 17. Explicit binding

Interfaces

An *interface* is another type of UML classifier used to define services that a class or component must provide. Interfaces are named according to the same rules as classes, but they contain only operations, not attributes. Interface names commonly begin with a capital I, as in IATAPIDevice.

In their expanded form, interfaces are drawn as stereotyped classes (see "Stereotypes") with an empty or omitted attribute compartment.

The distinction between operations and methods is particularly important with interfaces, as they may not include methods (operation implementations). Figure 18 shows the graphical representation of an interface in expanded form.

Figure 18. An expanded interface

Interfaces can also be represented in a more compact form as a simple circle. There is no specification difference between the two representations; they are used merely to distinguish interfaces from classes visually. The circle (or *icon*) representation is often used when showing interface realization (see "Classifier Relationships") in the stick-and-lollipop form. Figure 19 shows the icon representation of the interface shown earlier in Figure 18.

Figure 19. The icon version of an interface

It is common to have an interface define the services provided by a subsystem. In this case, a package (see "Packages") stereotyped as subsystem is shown realizing an interface. Some UML models actually make use of both class and subsystem realization of an interface, depending on the level of detail the particular class diagram is showing. Subsystem implementers may need to see exactly which classes realize the service defined by the interface, while clients of the service may only care which component or subsystem contains the requisite classes.

Strictly speaking, UML allows any visibility for operations defined for an interface. However, language mappings may require that interface methods be public.

Packages

Packages are all-purpose containers used to group related UML elements, including other packages. Packages are named according to the same convention as classes. Packages have a different graphical representation than classes; their names are located in the center of a folder, as shown in Figure 20.

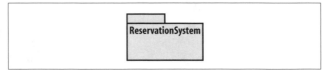

Figure 20. A sample package

While packages are typically used in class and component diagrams (which is why I chose to discuss them under the "Classes" heading), packages can actually be used to group just about anything.

Packages represent distinct namespaces within a model. Therefore, model elements owned by a package must have unique names within the package. However, those same names can be used for different elements in another package. UML also treats different types of elements, such as classes and components, as being in different namespaces, which means that a class may have the same name as a component regardless of whether they belong to the same package. However, giving two UML elements the same name is highly discouraged. Elements can be owned by only one package, but packages can access or import other packages.

Visibility of package elements

Packages introduce another level of visibility for contained elements. Each element within a package can be given one of the following levels of visibility:

public
> Indicates that the element can be used by anyone outside the package.

protected
> Indicates that the element can be used only by packages that inherit from the package.

private
> Indicates that the element can be used only by other elements contained within the same package.

Nested packages are considered to be within the same package and therefore can access *public*, *protected*, and *private* elements of their parent package. Note that this is different from Java's notion of packages.

Contents of a package, as well as their visibility, can be shown using the same folder icon. When showing the detailed contents of a package, the name of the package is moved to the folder tab and the package contents are shown within the folder. The contents can be shown as simple text, rectangles containing element names, or (rarely) using a graphical representation similar to the composition arrow. Figure 21 shows a textual representation of package contents.

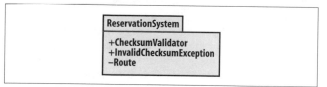

Figure 21. A package showing textual content and visibility

Figure 22 shows rectangular notation for package contents.

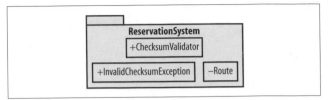

Figure 22. A package showing rectangular content notation

Figure 23 shows package contents using the UML anchor symbol.

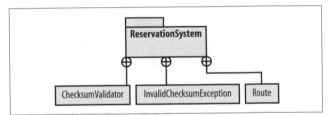

Figure 23. Package represented using composition-style notation

Visibility is shown using the standard +, #, and - symbols, for *public*, *protected*, and *private*, respectively. As with operations, some tools introduce ~ to show Java's default (*package-protected*) visibility.

Dependencies between packages

Packages almost always rely on other packages when used in a real system. Packages can relate to each other by depending on other packages or inheriting their elements. UML defines three stereotypes to refine package dependencies further:

Access

Shows that a package uses the public elements of another package but that each element must be fully qualified using the longer, colon-separated path name.

Import
> Shows that a package actually incorporates another package's public elements into its own namespace. This introduces possible naming conflicts, but it does not require elements to be scoped.

Friend
> Indicates that the dependent package is a friend package. A *friend* package can access all elements of the other package, regardless of visibility.

Typically, access and import are represented similarly in language mappings. Figure 24 shows sample package dependencies. ReservationSystem imports DBUtilities and uses elements in the AirlineNetworking package.

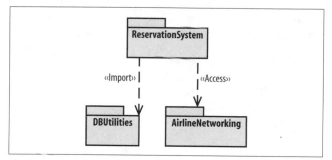

Figure 24. Package dependencies using stereotypes

Package inheritance

Packages inheriting from one another typically do not use stereotypes, and their behavior is similar to class inheritance. Package inheritance is represented using the same generalization relationship used for other types of elements, as shown in Figure 25.

Packages can replace public elements of their super-package with their own elements, as long as their elements adhere to the same interface contract as the elements being replaced. A

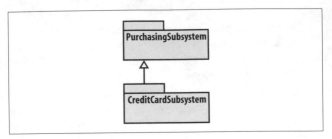

Figure 25. Package inheritance

package's protected elements are available to packages that inherit from it. However, private elements are still restricted to the containing package.

Packages are subject to the same replaceability requirements as classes. This means that if package B inherits from package A, package B must be usable anywhere package A can be used. Due to limited support by languages, package inheritance is seldom encountered.

Package stereotypes

There are five predefined UML stereotypes that are specific to packages:

Facade
> Used to indicate that a package is not a complete package, but rather a specific representation of another, larger package. The relationship between a facade package and the larger package is similar to the relationship between an interface and a class that implements that interface as well as other interfaces.

Framework
> Used to show that a package contains classes and interfaces that provide application-level patterns. These classes and interfaces are often used to implement subsystems within a larger application.

Stub

Used to show that a package does not contain the full implementation of a set of functionality; the package contains only the minimum requirements to define the service. Typically, a stub package contains interfaces, abstract classes, or proxy classes. Stub packages are deployed frequently on the client side of CORBA or EJB services.

Subsystem

Used to show that a package holds a self-contained set of functionality. A full system is often made up of several subsystems. Subsystems may depend on other subsystems but offer considerable functionality on their own. Subsystems are typically made up of multiple components.

System

Used to show that a package contains an entire system. This stereotype is typically used for a top-level package that contains several nested packages, further dividing the system into subsystems and components.

Figure 26 shows a package stereotyped as a subsystem.

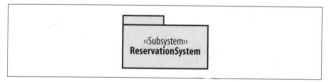

Figure 26. A stereotyped package

Package-tagged values

Packages support UML-tagged values. There are no pre-defined UML tags for packages. However, it is common to use tags for such things as author names, descriptions, versions, and external version requirements (such as

application major version 2.x). Figure 27 shows a package
with a version tag.

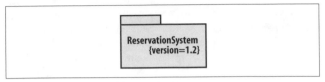

Figure 27. A package with tagged values

Classifier Relationships

Relationships between classes can be represented in several
ways, depending on the strength of the relationship.

Dependency

The weakest relationship is dependency. Dependencies are
used to indicate a loose coupling between two classes. Typically, a dependency represents a relationship in which the
class on the left side of the arrow briefly uses the class on the
right—for example, as a return type or parameter related to
an operation. Figure 28 shows an example of a simple class
dependency in which ChecksumValidator is dependent on
InvalidChecksumException.

Figure 28. A class dependency

Association

An association indicates a stronger relationship between two
classes than a dependency. Associations can indicate one- or
two-way navigation, depending on the presence of an arrow
showing the direction of navigability. An association line
with no arrows indicates two-way navigation. Classes bound
by associations have a persistent relationship that typically

exists longer than a single method call. Associations can be named at either or both ends to indicate the roles the association plays. As shown in Figure 29, the two instances of IDEBus are identified as mPrimaryIDE and mSecondaryIDE within one Motherboard.

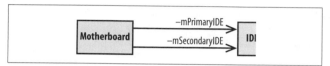

Figure 29. An association with roles

In addition to role names, associations can have constraints placed on them using the standard UML notation for constraints. See "Constraints" for more information on constraint syntax.

Multiplicity of each class in an association can be specified at the respective end of the association line. If no multiplicity is specified, 1 is assumed. Multiplicity in an association is specified in the same way as any other UML multiplicity: as a single number, as a range, or as comma-separated values. An asterisk (*) is used to represent any number. Figure 30 shows a multiplicity specification for an association that allows one Reservation to have one or more FlightLegs.

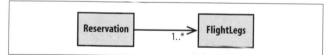

Figure 30. An association with multiplicity

Finally, associations can be named. Names are short phrases that help describe the relationship captured by an association. Names are usually applicable when reading an association in a certain direction, so UML allows placing a triangle at the appropriate end of the name to show the direction in which the name applies. Figure 31 shows a named association.

Figure 31. A named association

In Figure 31, the triangle indicates that the association name should be read from left to right, as Motherboard CommunicatesUsing IDEBus. Arrows are particularly helpful when layout constraints force you to present associations in an order that is different than the natural order for the language you are using.

Aggregation

Aggregation is a special type of association used to represent a "part of" relationship between two classes. The containing class is on the diamond side of the line, with the arrow pointing to the class that it contains. Like association, aggregation relationships can be bidirectional, though they are typically navigable only from the containing class to the contained class. A key indicator of an aggregate relationship is objects that share a lifetime. If the containing object is destroyed, the contained object is destroyed with it. Like associations, aggregations can be refined further with constraints, tagged values, and multiplicity indicators. Figure 32 shows an aggregation between two classes, indicating that a confirmation dialog contains an OK button.

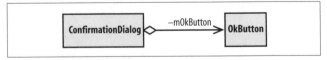

Figure 32. Aggregation relationships

Composition

Composition is the strongest relationship between two classes. Composition is a special form of aggregation that indicates not only lifetime association but typically exclusive containment as well. There is frequent debate over when composition is more appropriate than aggregation; some people argue that composition should never be used at all.

Frequently, composition is used to indicate exactly how a relationship should be represented in generated code. For example, in C++, aggregations are typically represented as pointers or references, while composition is typically represented by physically containing an instance of the aggregate class. In Java, composition is often used to show relationships with inner classes. Like aggregations, composition relationships can be refined with constraints, tagged values, and multiplicity indicators. Figure 33 shows class composition.

Figure 33. A composition relationship

Generalization

Generalization is used to show inheritance: subclass B has an "is a" relationship with superclass A, or superclass A is a generalization of subclass B. A single class can inherit from multiple superclasses, though this might not be supported by the language mappings. For example, C++ supports multiple inheritance, while Java does not. Generalization does not require the more specific class to provide operation implementations, so an interface can inherit another interface. Figure 34 shows a generalization relationship between two classes, indicating that FlightReservation inherits from Reservation.

Realization

Realization indicates that a class implements (or *realizes*) the interface pointed to by a realization arrow. Much like inheritance, realization indicates that the class realizing an interface is an implementation of the referenced interface. While interfaces define only operation signatures, a realization ties an

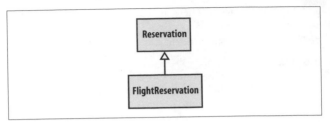

Figure 34. Class generalization

interface to a concrete implementation (e.g., to a concrete set of methods). It is not uncommon to show packages (stereotyped as subsystems) realizing subsystem interfaces. A single class can realize multiple interfaces. Since interfaces cannot have implementations, an interface cannot realize another interface. Figure 35 shows a class realizing an interface.

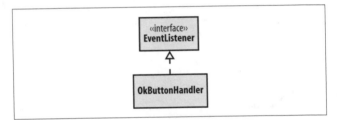

Figure 35. Interface realization

UML defines an alternate representation of interface realization, named the *stick-and-lollipop* notation, as shown in Figure 36.

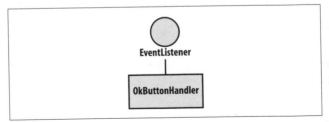

Figure 36. Stick-and-lollipop notation for interfaces

Object Diagrams

Object diagrams show the relationship between instances of UML elements. Most UML elements represent abstract types or relationships between types. Concrete instances of classes are objects, while concrete instances of relationships are links. Each abstract UML element has an associated concrete-instance element.

Objects

Objects are concrete instances of classes. All objects must be either uniquely named or anonymous. The name of an object is followed by a colon, then the name of the type. The entire object name, including its type, is underlined. Anonymous objects have no name; however, the colon must be present and the colon and class name are underlined. Object names follow the same rules as class names. The name of an object can be a simple name or a fully qualified path name. Figure 37 shows both anonymous and named objects.

Figure 37. Anonymous and named objects

Multiobjects

Multiple objects of the same type can be represented as UML multiobjects, as shown in Figure 38.

Figure 38. Multiobjects

Orphaned objects

Though rarely used, UML also allows for objects without an associated abstraction or class. Such an object is called an *orphaned object* and is represented only by its object name and the colon, as shown in Figure 39.

Figure 39. An orphaned object

Object methods

Whereas an object is an instance of a class, a method is an instance of an operation. The UML notation for invoking an operation on an object is as follows:

```
classname.operationName( )
```

Depending on the inheritance tree of the abstraction and use of adornments such as final, the operation may be polymorphic.

Object attributes and states

Since objects are instances of a class, objects have attributes. However, unlike classes, objects also have states. The state of an object can be represented by showing the value of its attributes at a given time. The types of the attributes can be omitted, since the abstraction class provides the necessary type information. Figure 40 shows the state of a returnTrip object. Notice that a type is specified for one attribute and elided for the other.

returnTrip : Reservation
airlineName : String = "US Air" departureTime = 0830UTC

Figure 40. The state of an object using attributes

Because objects are part of an executing system, showing the state of an object is simply a snapshot of attribute values at a certain time. An object's state can be captured more abstractly using a textual representation of an explicit state. Figure 41 shows the same returnTrip object with the explicit state of Confirmed.

Figure 41. An object with an explicit state

When using the notation style shown in Figure 41, you can list multiple states if an object is in more than one state at a given time. For example, if the reservation was both confirmed and paid for, you might list the states as [Confirmed, paid-for].

While objects and object diagrams can be used to show object states and state transitions, it is more common to use a state diagram to capture this information. See "Statechart Diagrams" for more information.

Active and passive objects

UML provides notation to distinguish between active and passive objects. Active objects are used in conjunction with multithreaded or multiprocesser systems to identify objects that initiate activity with other objects. Typically, each active object maps to a distinct thread or process within the system. Active objects are represented using a wider rectangle, as shown in Figure 42.

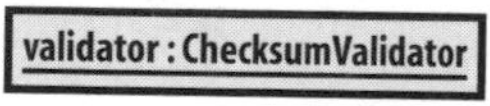

validator : ChecksumValidator

Figure 42. An active object

Object Stereotypes

Typically, objects are not stereotyped; instead, they take the stereotype of the associated abstraction class. There are several stereotypes that apply to dependencies and links between objects. See "Stereotypes" for a detailed list of applicable standard stereotypes.

Object Modeling

Just as objects are instances of classes, object diagrams are instances of class diagrams. Object diagrams show the static relationships between objects for a particular snapshot of a running system. Object diagrams consist of objects, links between objects, notes, and constraints. Packages can be used to group related objects, but this is uncommon. Figure 43 shows an object diagram that includes the values of attributes at the time of the snapshot.

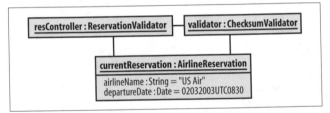

Figure 43. A sample object diagram

As mentioned earlier, links are instantiations of associations and therefore can have directionality, names, roles, and stereotypes. See "Stereotypes" for a list of standard stereotypes that can be applied to links.

Component Diagrams

Component diagrams are similar to class diagrams but concentrate on higher, subsystem-level abstractions. Component

---

diagrams typically contain components, interfaces, and their relationships.

Components

A *component* is a physical piece of a system, such as a compiled object file, piece of source code, shared library, or Enterprise Java Bean (EJB). Figure 44 shows the default representation for a component. Like classes, the name of a component can be fully qualified using :: to separate package names.

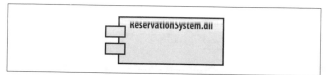

Figure 44. A simple component

UML allows users to replace the default representation of a UML element when using stereotypes. For example, rather than use the icon shown in Figure 44, modeling tools typically use a dog-eared piece of paper to represent a component stereotyped as a document. Customized representations of UML elements are frequently used in component diagrams, as UML provides standard stereotypes, though not icons, for the following types of components:

document
> The stereotyped component represents some type of textual document (Word, text, RTF, etc.).

executable
> The stereotyped component represents a complete executable that can be run on a node.

file
> The stereotyped component represents some type of file, such as source code, system data, input, or output.

`library`
The stereotyped component represents a shared or static library of compiled code.

`table`
The stereotyped component represents a database table.

Components can have multiple compartments to further expose information, such as interfaces the component realizes or classes contained in an EJB archive. Figure 45 shows a component with a compartment that displays contained classes.

Figure 45. A component showing contained classes within a compartment

Alternatively, contained classes can be represented using dependencies, as shown in Figure 46.

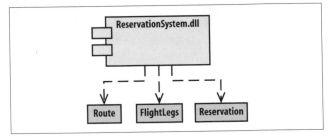

Figure 46. An alternate view of contained classes, using dependencies

Components can have operations listed on them, but the operations are typically available only through the interfaces they realize. UML allows for components to have attributes, but you won't see this often. Information such as manifest values in a Java *.jar* file are more appropriately modeled as tagged values, as shown in Figure 47.

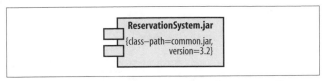

Figure 47. A component showing manifest values in a .jar file

Component Modeling

Like class diagrams, component diagrams are used to show the static assembly of a system. Component diagrams can show how subsystems relate and which interfaces are implemented by which components. Associations, generalizations, dependencies, and realizations can be used in component diagrams, as shown in Figure 48.

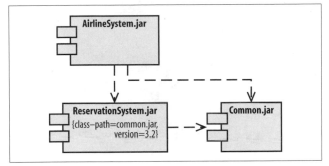

Figure 48. A sample component diagram

Typically, a component diagram shows one or more interfaces and their relationships to other components. Interfaces are central to component-based development and modeling, so they are usually the focus of component diagrams. A component-interface relationship can be represented with the graphic stick-and-lollipop representation, as shown in Figure 49.

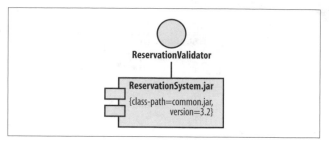

Figure 49. Interface realization using stick-and-lollipop notation

Interface realization can also be represented using the standard realization arrow used in class diagrams, as shown in Figure 50.

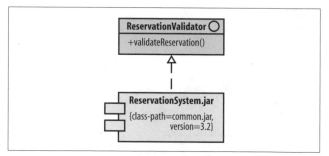

Figure 50. Interface realization using the realization arrow

More typically, components and interfaces are included in the same diagram to illustrate interface realization and the dependencies of other components on those interfaces. Technically, component-to-component dependency is a component-to-interface dependency, plus a realization to the component implementing the interface. Dependency is represented using the same arrow used for class dependency, as shown in Figure 51.

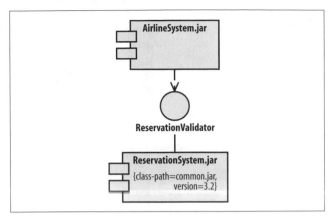

Figure 51. Interface realization and component dependencies

Deployment Diagrams

Deployment diagrams show the physical nodes on which a system executes. Deployment diagrams typically contain nodes, components, and the associations between the nodes and components.

Nodes

A *node* is a physical entity that executes one or more components, subsystems, or executables (though, strictly speaking, subsystems and executables are simply stereotyped components). A node is rendered as a cube and, like all other UML classifiers, has a name that is unique within its package. Figure 52 shows a simple node.

Nodes can have multiple named compartments that show extra information, such as deployed components, as shown in Figure 53. Attributes and operations can be specified for nodes.

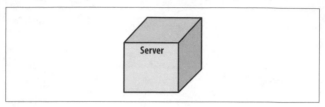

Figure 52. A node

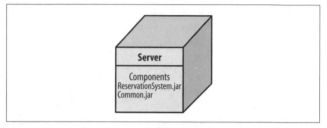

Figure 53. A node with multiple compartments

Rather than list contents of a node in a compartment, you can represent deployed components using dependency relations between the node and the components, as shown in Figure 54.

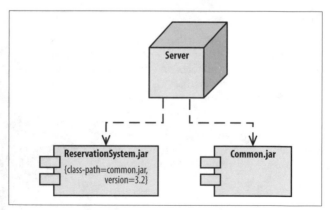

Figure 54. A node with its deployed components

Node Modeling

Relationships between nodes are represented as associations and can be stereotyped to capture additional information. While UML allows for all association types (e.g., composition, aggregation, and simple associations) to be used for nodes, the simple association line is usually used. Associations between nodes are called *connections*. Figure 55 shows three nodes and their connections.

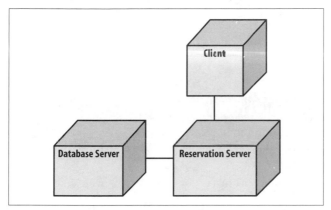

Figure 55. Multiple nodes and their connections

Like classes and components, nodes can be organized within packages. Typically, nodes are stereotyped and rendered using custom icons when modeling anything but the simplest system. Common node stereotypes include database, server, client, and backup server, though UML does not provide any standard stereotypes for nodes. Figure 56 shows a typical deployment diagram using stereotyped nodes.

Behavioral Diagrams

Behavioral diagrams are used to capture the dynamic execution of a system, including required functionality, state

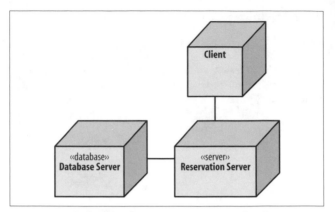

Figure 56. A deployment diagram using stereotyped nodes

transitions within classes, components, entire subsystems, and object interactions. Behavioral diagrams can show the flow of execution in a system, including simple object interactions, component migration, or complex multithreaded system flows.

Behavioral modeling encompasses the following diagrams:

- Use case diagrams
- Sequence and interaction diagrams
- Collaboration diagrams
- Statechart diagrams
- Activity diagrams

The various behavioral diagrams are closely related. For example, sequence diagrams can be created from collaboration diagrams and vice versa. Behavioral diagrams are also closely linked with static diagrams. Class diagrams show realizations of the requirements captured in use case diagrams, and sequence diagrams show the interactions of objects shown in object diagrams.

Use Case Diagrams

Use case diagrams are used to capture the requirements of a system. The term *use case* is often used to refer to a document that describes a particular piece of functionality a system must provide. Strictly speaking, however, a use case is a UML element, and the document describing a use case is a *use case document*. Throughout this section, the term *use case* refers to the UML notion of a use case and not to the document.

Use Cases

Typically, use cases are short phrases or sentences that sum up a distinct piece of functionality a system offers a user. Like other UML elements, use cases are often grouped into packages and can be referenced using their fully qualified name. Along with the name of a use case, there is a sequence of events that describe the behavior of the system when the use case is invoked. UML does not define a notation for recording the sequence of events for a use case, so the sequence is often described in a separate use case document, which is simply a text document created using any word-processing program. A use case is represented in a use case diagram by an ellipse, as shown in Figure 57.

Figure 57. A use case

Use cases are at a higher level of abstraction than other UML elements and describe, from the user's perspective, functionality a system must provide. Use cases do not specify how the system actually implements the functionality. Use cases are intended to communicate desired functionality from end users to project managers and actual developers.

Actors

Use cases are associated with one or more actors. An actor is a role a user takes when invoking a use case. Since a user can fulfill multiple roles, a single user can be represented by multiple actors. Likewise, a single actor can represent multiple users. An actor is represented as a stick figure with the name of the actor written underneath, as shown in Figure 58.

Figure 58. An actor

Actors do not always need to represent human users. Actors can be used to represent external systems with which a modeled system interacts. For example, you might model a robotic-tape subsystem as an actor. Actors help draw the boundary between what needs to be implemented as part of the system being modeled and what exists outside of the system.

Use cases and actors are connected using associations. When using associations on use case diagrams, the directionality of the association indicates only who initiates the interaction, not the direction of information flow. For example, Figure 59 shows both human and machine systems interacting with a use case from an ATM system. Obviously, there is interaction with the customer while the withdrawal takes place; however, the ATM never initiates a withdrawal by contacting the user.

Figure 59. Human and machine actors and use cases

A bidirectional association indicates functionality that can be invoked by either the system or the actor.

Use Case Modeling

Use cases often relate to other use cases within the same system. Use cases are related using generalization, extension, or inclusion.

Use case generalization

Use case generalization behaves exactly like class generalization; a specialized use case inherits the behavior of the original use case. The specialized use case can then replace or enhance the behavior, but it adheres to the external contracts of the original use case. Generalization is modeled using the same generalization arrow used with classes, as shown in Figure 60.

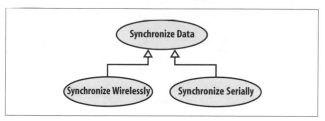

Figure 60. Use case generalization

Use case inclusion

A use case can include the behavior of another use case. The included use case is not used by itself; it can be used only in a part of a larger, separate use case. Most often, use case inclusion is used when pulling out common functionality that is shared between use cases. When including another use case, the containing use case explicitly states in its flow of events when the included use case is invoked. For example, an online purchasing system may include a use case to authenticate customers within a larger use case for purchasing an item. In this example, customer authentication would never happen outside of the context of the larger goal.

Use case inclusion is shown using a dependency arrow that is stereotyped with `include`, as shown in Figure 61.

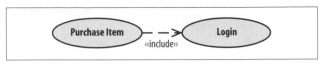

Figure 61. Use case inclusion

Use case extension

Use case extension is used to encapsulate a distinct flow of events that are not considered part of the normal or basic flow. They are not necessarily exceptional conditions, but they are sufficiently large parts of functionality that incorporating them in the base use case detracts from the focus of that use case.

When using a use case extension, the author of the base use case document explicitly states the points at which the base use case can be extended by other use cases. Unlike included use cases, extension use cases can be complete, standalone use cases that simply plug into a larger system at defined extension points in the base use case. For example, the previously mentioned online-purchasing system cannot log all communication involved in placing an order unless it is in some sort of debugging mode. The `Purchase Item` use case can be extended by a separate `Log Debugging Info` use case if the debugging criteria are met.

Use case extension is modeled using a dependency arrow stereotyped with `extend` and named with the name of the extension point, as shown in Figure 62.

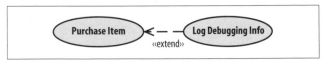

Figure 62. Use case extension

Use Case Realization

Since use cases capture requirements at a functional level, UML provides a mechanism for tracing functional requirements to their actual implementation. This mapping is called *use case realization*. Like interface realization, use case realization is shown using the realization arrow between a collaboration and a use case. A collaboration looks like a use case ellipse drawn with a dashed line, and it is typically linked to one or more UML diagrams. Figure 63 shows an example of a collaboration in a use case realization.

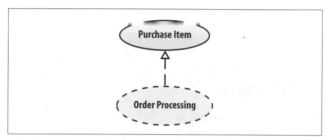

Figure 63. A use case realization

Typically, a single collaboration draws in elements from multiple packages and contains its own diagrams that show how these elements interact to provide the required functionality. Collaborations call on both static and behavioral diagrams to show how a use case is implemented. Diagrams within a collaboration often stop at subsystem or interface boundaries, in which case the details of subsystem functionality are left to subsystem modeling.

Collaborations can relate to other collaborations in that one collaboration provides more detail in a particular area than another collaboration. Thus, one collaboration may be dependent on another. To model collaboration relationships, use a dependency arrow stereotyped as refine. Figure 64 shows that the Order Distribution collaboration refines the Order Processing collaboration.

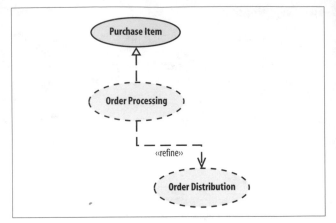

Figure 64. Collaboration refinement

Use Case Documents

While technically not part of UML, use case documents are closely related to UML use cases. A use case document is text that captures the detailed functionality of a use case. Such documents typically contain the following parts:

Brief description

Used to describe the overall intent of the use case. Typically, the brief description is only a few paragraphs, but it can be longer or shorter as needed. It describes what is considered the *happy path*—the functionality that occurs when the use case executes without errors. It can include critical variations on the happy path, if needed.

Precondititons

Conditionals that must be true before the use case can begin to execute. Note that this means the author of the use case document does not need to check these conditions during the basic flow, as they must be true for the basic flow to begin.

Basic flow

Used to capture the normal flow of execution through the use case. The basic flow is often represented as a numbered list that describes the interaction between an actor and the system. Decision points in the basic flow branch off to alternate flows. Use case extension points and inclusions are typically documented in the basic flow.

Alternate flows

Used to capture variations to the basic flows, such as user decisions or error conditions. There are typically multiple alternate flows in a single use case. Some alternate flows rejoin the basic flow at a specified point, while others terminate the use case.

Postconditions

Conditionals that must be true for the use case to complete. Postconditions are typically used by testers to verify that the realization of the use case is implemented correctly.

Sequence and Collaboration Diagrams

Sequence and collaboration diagrams are tightly related. Both show a time-based flow of messages between objects; they differ only in how the information is presented. Most UML tools can create one from the other without user intervention. Collaboration diagrams emphasize the relationships between objects, while sequence diagrams emphasize the sequential, time-based nature of message passing.

Collaboration Diagrams

Collaboration diagrams capture the flow of control during the execution of some part of system behavior. The collaboration diagram can represent behavior within a single class, a component, or an entire use case.

Collaboration diagrams use the same building blocks used by object diagrams: objects, components, use case realizations, and links over which messages are sent. However, collaboration diagrams label each link with information that shows the direction and type of message sent between elements. Technically, abstract classes and interfaces cannot be instantiated directly; still, it is not uncommon to see both used on collaboration diagrams. Interfaces or abstract classes on collaboration diagrams represent instantiations of a realizing or concrete class. Since interfaces and abstract classes carry with them contracts for behavior, the interface or abstract class can be used to represent an arbitrary implementation.

A link in a collaboration diagram is usually adorned with a sequence number that shows the order in which the message occurs, the name of the operation being invoked, and an arrow indicating the direction the message flows. Figure 65 shows typical links in a collaboration diagram.

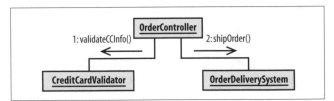

Figure 65. A simple collaboration diagram

To further clarify relationships between objects, you can stereotype the end of a link with one of the following stereotypes:

Association
> The object at the end of the link is visible due to the association.

Self
> The object at the end of the link is the same object as the sender of the message.

Global
> The object at the end of the link is global in an enclosing scope.

Local
:   The object at the end of the link is part of a local scope.

Parameter
:   The object at the end of the link is visible because it is a parameter.

Sequence Diagrams

As mentioned earlier, a sequence diagram is simply a different rendering of a collaboration diagram. Rather than emphasize the connectivity between objects, a sequence diagram emphasizes the time-based flow of events. A sequence diagram shows the participating objects along the top of the diagram, with messages listed from top to bottom in order of execution. Figure 66 shows a sequence diagram of the object collaboration in Figure 65.

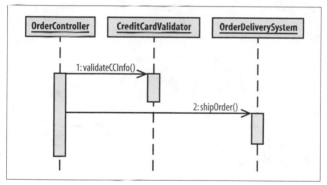

Figure 66. A simple sequence diagram

Object creation and deletion

Objects created during the time covered by a sequence diagram are often shown directly above the message that creates them. Figure 67 shows object creation in sequence-diagram form.

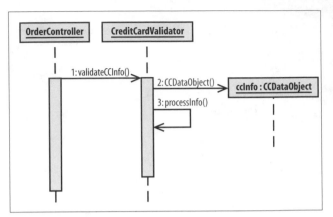

Figure 67. A sequence diagram showing object creation

Likewise, objects destroyed during the time covered by a sequence usually are not drawn beyond the message that causes the destruction. The lifeline of the object is terminated with an X, as shown in Figure 68.

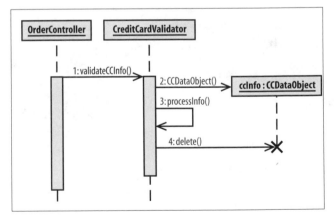

Figure 68. A sequence diagram showing object destruction

Object messages

Each message passed to an object invokes some type of response, called an *action*. UML predefines five actions: call, return, send, create, and destroy.

Call is used to indicate that the message is an invocation of an operation on the target object. An object can call an operation on itself, in which case the operation is modeled as a link back to the object. The link can be stereotyped with self to add clarity to the model. A message that results in an operation invocation is named for the operation that is invoked. UML allows you to specify arguments to the operation as part of the message name; however, most UML tools do not support this call is represented as a filled arrow, as shown in Figure 69.

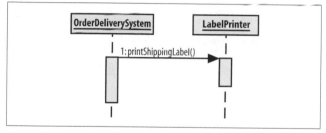

Figure 69. A sample call message

Return is a special type of message that indicates the result of a previous call to an operation. Return is represented as a dashed line that ends with an arrow pointing to the object receiving the return value. The link is often named for the object that is returned. Return values from calls are not usually shown in interaction diagrams, but they may be found on sequence diagrams, as shown in Figure 70.

Send indicates that a message is actually a signal to the receiving object. Signals are asynchronous communications between two objects or components. Signals are represented by a solid line that ends with half an arrow, as shown in Figure 71.

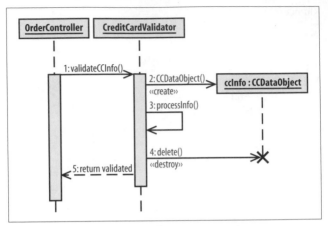

Figure 70. A sequence diagram showing return values

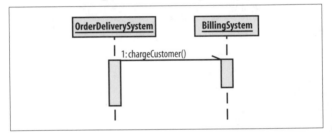

Figure 71. A signal in a sequence diagram

Create indicates that the target object is being instantiated as a result of a message. Typically, create is used to represent a call to new in Java or C++. Create is represented as a stereotype on a basic message.

Destroy indicates that the target object is destroyed as a result of a message. An object can send a destroy message to itself to indicate that the object terminates itself. Destroy is usually mapped to delete in C++. While Java does not have an explicit delete keyword, the destroy action is used to indicate that the target object is dereferenced and is considered garbage by the system. Delete is represented as a stereotyped message with an X at the end of the arrow, as shown in Figure 72.

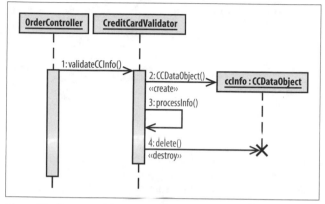

Figure 72. Create and destroy actions in a sequence diagram

You can add new action types as needed; new action types can be represented as stereotypes on basic messages or explained further using UML notes.

Statechart Diagrams

Statechart diagrams are used to show the various stages (or *states*) an entity may be in during its lifetime. A statechart diagram can be used to show the state transitions of methods, objects, components, subsystems, or entire systems.

States

A state represents a condition of a modeled entity for which some action is performed, some stimulus is received, or some condition elsewhere in a system is met. Typically, an entity remains in a state for a measurable amount of time; however, UML supports modeling of instantaneous states to help model a flow of operation.

Each state is rendered as a rectangle with round corners. The name of a state can be shown as a tab attached to the top of the state; however, this is usually used only for composite states (see "Composite States"). Like classes, state names are usually rendered in a name compartment, as shown in Figure 73.

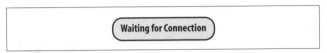

Figure 73. A state

Actions and Activities

States can have a second compartment that contains actions or activities performed while an entity is in a given state. An *action* is an atomic execution and therefore completes without interruption. An *activity* is a more complex collection of behavior that may run for a long duration. An activity may be interrupted by events, in which case it does not run to completion. Each action or activity can have an *action label* defining an event that causes the action or activity to trigger. UML predefines four action labels:

entry
    The specified action triggers upon entering the state.

exit
    The specified action triggers upon exiting the state.

do
    The specified action triggers after an entry action and runs until completion or an externally triggered state transition. Note that completion of the action may trigger an event that causes the entity to leave the state.

include
    The specified action refers to another statechart (a *submachine*) that contains other, internal states (or *substates*).

The syntax for an action label and action is as follows:

```
action-label-or-event (parameters)
[guard-condition]/action-expression
```

This syntax contains the following user-defined elements:

action-label-or-event
> An action or event that triggers the action described in *action-expression*.

parameters
> Objects or values made available to the action. Typically, *parameters* are attributes of the event triggering the action, or the enclosing object represented by the state machine.

guard-condition
> A Boolean expression indicating some additional criteria that must be met before the action specified by *action-expression* can occur.

action-expression
> A representation of the behavior that occurs as a result of the trigger event. The behavior can be described in natural language, pseudocode, or real code expressions.

Figure 74 shows a state with multiple actions.

Figure 74. A state with multiple actions

Transitions

The initial state of a state machine is represented as a solid, black circle, connected by a transition to the first state of an entity. Transitions between states are represented as directed arcs between states. Like states, transitions can have events and actions. A transition can be labeled with the event or action that creates the entity.

The final state of a state machine is represented as a circle around a filled dot. This state indicates the completion of a state machine and can trigger a completion event in an enclosing composite state. Figure 75 shows a complete state machine.

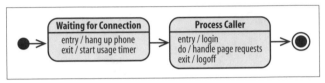

Figure 75. A complete state machine

Composite States

A composite state is made up of other substates and is shown with states and state transitions contained inside. Technically, a statechart diagram is a composite state that represents a state machine of a modeled entity. However, the outermost, composite state is not usually shown.

A composite state can be subdivided into multiple concurrent state machines, known as *submachines*. Each submachine is separated from the others by a dashed line. The name of the composite state is separated with a solid line, as shown in Figure 76.

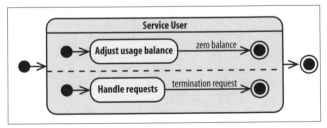

Figure 76. Concurrent state machines

Concurrent state machines are frequently used to model concurrent threads within a larger system.

Sync States

UML supports a special type of state named a sync state. A *sync state* is used in a concurrent state machine to indicate that the associated concurrent transitions must meet up (or *sync*) before entering the next state. A sync state is represented as an asterisk in a circle, as shown in Figure 77 in the next section.

Concurrent Transitions

To support concurrent states, UML allows for concurrent transitions. Concurrent transitions represent either forking or joining when transitioning between states. A concurrent transition is represented by a thick, solid line with one or more transition lines leading to the next state or states. Figure 77 shows concurrent transitions, demonstrating both forking and joining.

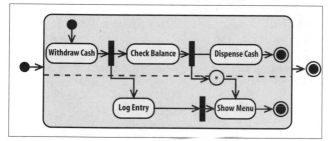

Figure 77. Concurrent transitions

In Figure 77, the transition out of the Withdraw Cash state makes both Check Balance and Log Entry concurrent. Then, both Log Entry and Check Balance must complete before Show Menu becomes current.

Activity Diagrams

Much like state diagrams, activity diagrams are used to capture behavioral flow information. However, activity diagrams concentrate on transitions between states without showing external stimuli. State transitions within an activity diagram occur simply because of the completion of actions associated with previous states.

Activity diagrams capture state transitions for a given entity, such as a class, operation, use case, or subsystem, and are frequently used to model algorithms or procedures. Like state diagrams, activity diagrams have an initial state shown as a filled circle and a final state shown as a filled circle with a ring around it.

Action States

An activity diagram is made up of multiple action states. An *action state* represents a state with an entry action and an implicit transition to the next state. An action state can have a guard condition that restricts transition to the next state. An action state is represented as a rectangle with rounded sides. The action associated with the state is simply written in the rectangle. The action can be written as a short phrase or as pseudocode. When using pseudocode, you can reference attributes or links of the owning entity. Figure 78 shows an example of an action state.

> **Submit Requisition**

Figure 78. An action state

Transitions

A transition between action states is represented as a straight line that ends with an arrow pointing to the next

---

state. Transitions cannot have events associated with them, but they can have guard conditions. Figure 79 shows several action states and the transitions between them.

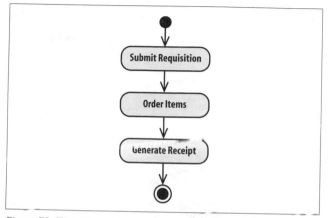

Figure 79. Transitions between action states

Subactivity State

A subactivity state is used to embed a separate activity diagram within a larger diagram. Upon entering a subactivity state, the initial action state of the subactivity diagram is entered. After completing the final action state of the subactivity diagram, execution resumes with the state that follows the subactivity state.

A subactivity state is rendered like an action state, but with an icon representing an activity diagram in the lower right, as shown in Figure 80. Details of the subactivity state would be shown on a separate activity diagram.

Figure 80. A subactivity state

Decision and Merge

A single transition from a state can split into multiple transitions, depending on guard conditions. Decision points in an activity diagram are shown as diamonds; a single transition enters each diamond and multiple transitions come out. UML predefines one guard condition, else, which can be used if all the guard conditions can be false. Figure 81 shows a decision that results in different action states.

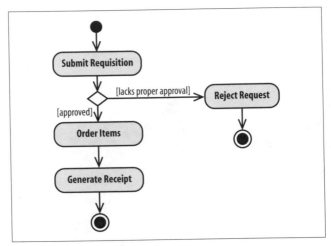

Figure 81. A decision in an activity diagram

After a decision, the various paths through an activity diagram can join into one path through a merge. A merge is also shown as a diamond, but it has multiple transitions leading into the diamond and only one leading out. The transition leading out of the diamond cannot have a guard condition. Figure 82 shows several action states merging into one action state.

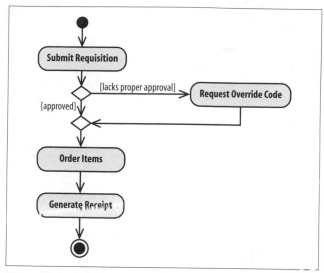

Figure 82. A merge in an activity diagram

Call States

A call state is simply an action state in which the behavior is exactly one call action. In other words, the action associated with a call state maps directly to an operation on an entity. A call state is rendered in the same way as an action state; the name of the operation is shown in the state and the entity owning the operation is shown in parenthesis under the operation. Call states are used when you want to be explicit about what happens during an activity diagram. An activity diagram using call states is similar to a sequence diagram. Figure 83 shows a call state.

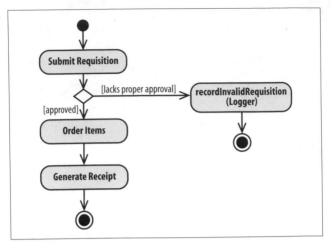

Figure 83. A call state

Swimlanes

An activity diagram can be divided into multiple vertical partitions called *swimlanes*. At the top of each swimlane, you can place a label that indicates how the activities in the swimlane are related. Swimlanes do not necessarily indicate which object or component carries out a given activity. They are used to capture how activities fit together in a higher, business-level workflow. Each swimlane is separated from the others by solid, vertical lines. Transitions can cross swimlanes freely. Figure 84 shows an activity diagram divided into swimlanes.

Participating Objects

Objects involved in an action state, either as input objects or as output objects, can be represented using dependency arrows. Objects that provide input to an action are shown

---

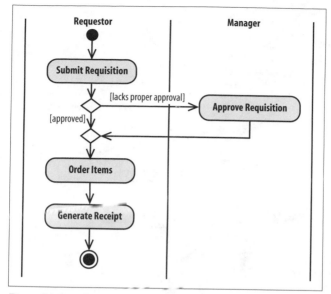

Figure 84. Swimlanes in an activity diagram

with a dependency on the action state. An object that is the result of an action state is shown with a dependency arrow from the action state to the object. You can label the state of an object explicitly by placing the name of the state in brackets after the name of an object. This is helpful when using the object as input or output from multiple states. Figure 85 shows an object involved in an activity diagram.

Signals

The sending and receiving of signals are common occurrences in an activity diagram. UML provides two symbols to use with signals. The first indicates receipt of a signal: the name of the signal is written on a rectangle that has a concave

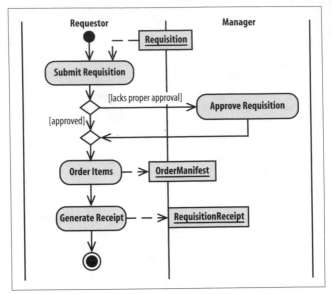

Figure 85. Object participating in an activity diagram

triangle on one side of it. Signal reception is represented as part of an activity diagram by showing a transition from a previous state to the signal symbol, followed by a transition to the next state. You can show the object that sent the signal as an object on the activity diagram with a dependency on the signal reception symbol.

The second signal symbol, a rectangle with a convex triangle at one end, indicates transmission of a signal. Placement in an activity diagram is the same as with signal reception. You can represent the receiver by showing a dependency from the signal symbol to the object receiving the signal.

Figure 86 shows the sending and receiving of signals in an activity diagram.

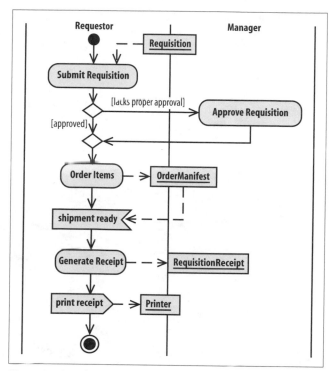

Figure 86. Signals in an activity diagram

Index

Symbols

:: (double colon), specifying fully qualified names, 17, 41

(...) (ellipse)
 eliding operations/ attributes, 16, 20
 representing use cases, 49

(hash mark), showing protected visibility
 of attributes, 18
 of operations, 20
 of package elements, 28

- (minus sign), showing private visibility
 of attributes, 18
 of operations, 20
 of package elements, 28

+ (plus sign), showing public visibility
 of attributes, 18
 of operations, 20
 of package elements, 28

A

abstract classes on collaboration diagrams, 56
abstract operations, 22

access stereotype, 5, 28
action labels, 62
 syntax for, 63
action states, 66–71
 merging, 68
 objects involved in, 70
 transitions between, 66
action types for objects, 59
actions/activities in statechart diagrams, 62
active and passive objects, distinguishing between, 39
activity diagrams
 action states in, 66–71
 call states in, 69
 decision points in, 68
 merging action states, 68
 signals in, 71–73
 subactivity states in, 67
 swimlanes in, 70
actor stereotype, 5
actors in use cases, 50
aggregation relationships between classes, 34
alternate flows in use case documents, 55
anonymous objects, 37

Other Titles Available from O'Reilly

UML

Learning UML

By Sinan Si Alhir
1st Edition July 2003 (est.)
304 pages (est.), ISBN 0-596-00344-7

Learning UML starts with the foundational concepts of object-orientation in order to provide the proper context for explaining UML. This language includes several diagram types, and complete chapters in this book have been devoted to each, with a common case study example used throughout to provide unity. The mechanics of generating correct UML diagrams, and how those diagrams can be put to practical use, are explained.

UML in a Nutshell

By Sinan Si Alhir
1st Edition September 1998
286 pages, 1-56592-448-7

The Unified Modeling Language (UML), for the first time in the history of systems engineering, gives practitioners a common language. This concise quick reference explains how to use each component of the language, including its extension mechanisms and the Object Constraint Language (OCL). A tutorial with realistic examples brings those new to the UML quickly up to speed.

C++ in a Nutshell

By Ray Lischner
1st Edition May 2003
840 pages, ISBN 0-596-00298-x

C++ in a Nutshell is a quick reference to the most important and most often used aspects of C++. The book's library reference is organized by header file, and each library chapter and class declaration presents the classes and types in alphabetical order, for easy lookup. Cross-references link related methods, classes, and other key features.

C++ Pocket Reference

By Kyle Loudon
1st Edition June 2003
144 pages, ISBN 0-596-00496-6

C++ Pocket Reference is a highly focused reference to the most vital and often-used aspects necessary for writing good, clean applications. Included is an introduction to C++, followed by short sections on topics such as classes, data types and memory management, with pointed examples and a brief list of tips.

Java in a Nutshell, 4th Edition

By David Flanagan
4th Edition March 2002
992 pages, ISBN 0-596-00283-1

This bestselling quick reference contains an accelerated introduction to the Java programming language and its key APIs, so seasoned programmers can start writing Java code right away. The fourth edition of *Java in a Nutshell* covers the new Java 1.4 beta edition, which contains significant changes from the 1.3 version.

Unix Basics

Learning the UNIX Operating System, 5th Edition

By Jerry Peek, Grace Todino
& John Strang
5th Edition October 2001
176 pages, ISBN 0-596-00261-0

Learning the UNIX Operating System is the most effective introduction to Unix in print. The fifth edition covers Internet usage for email, file transfers, and web browsing. It's perfect for those who are just starting with Unix or Linux, as well as anyone who encounters a Unix system on the Internet. Complete with a quick-reference card to pull out and keep handy, it's an ideal primer for Mac and PC users of the Internet who need to know a little bit about Unix on the systems they visit.

Learning the Korn Shell, 2nd Edition

By Bill Rosenblatt, Arnold Robbins
2nd Edition April 2002
432 pages, ISBN 0-596-00195-9

Learning the Korn Shell is the key to gaining control of the Korn shell and becoming adept at using it as an interactive command and scripting language. Readers will learn how to write many applications more easily and quickly than with other high-level languages. A solid offering for many years, this newly revised title inherits a long tradition of trust among computer professionals who want to learn or refine an essential skill.

O'REILLY®

To order: *800-998-9938* • *order@oreilly.com* • *www.oreilly.com*
Online editions of most O'Reilly titles are available by subscription at *safari.oreilly.com*
Also available at most retail and online bookstores.

UNIX in a Nutshell: System V Edition, 3rd Edition

By Arnold Robbins
3rd Edition September 1999
616 pages, ISBN 1-56592-427-4

The bestselling, most informative Unix reference book is now more complete and up-to-date. Not a scaled-down quick reference of common commands, *UNIX in a Nutshell* is a complete reference containing all commands and options, with descriptions and examples that put the commands in context. For all but the thorniest Unix problems, this one reference should be all you need. Covers System V Release 4 and Solaris 7.

Using csh and tcsh

By Paul DuBois
1st Edition August 1995
242 pages, ISBN 1-56592-132-1

Using csh and tcsh describes from the beginning how to use these shells interactively to get your work done faster with less typing. You'll learn how to make your prompt tell you where you are (no more pwd); use what you've typed before (history); type long command lines with few keystrokes (command and filename completion); remind yourself of filenames when in the middle of typing a command; and edit a botched command without retyping it.

Learning GNU Emacs, 2nd Edition

By Debra Cameron, Bill Rosenblatt & Eric Raymond
2nd Edition September 1996
560 pages, ISBN 1-56592-152-6

Learning GNU Emacs is an introduction to Version 19.30 of the GNU Emacs editor, one of the most widely used and powerful editors available under Unix. It provides a solid introduction to basic editing, a look at several important "editing modes" (special Emacs features for editing specific types of documents, including email, Usenet News, and the World Wide Web), and a brief introduction to customization and Emacs LISP programming. The book is aimed at new Emacs users, whether or not they are programmers. Includes quick-reference card.

Learning the vi Editor, 6th Edition

By Linda Lamb & Arnold Robbins
6th Edition October 1998
348 pages, ISBN 1-56592-426-6

This completely updated guide to editing with vi, the editor available on nearly every Unix system, now covers four popular vi clones and includes command summaries for easy reference. It starts with the basics, followed by more advanced editing tools, such as ex commands, global search and replacement, and a new feature, multi-screen editing.

O'REILLY®

To order: *800-998-9938* • *order@oreilly.com* • *www.oreilly.com*
Online editions of most O'Reilly titles are available by subscription at *safari.oreilly.com*
Also available at most retail and online bookstores.

Learning the bash Shell, 2nd Edition

By Cameron Newham
& Bill Rosenblatt
2nd Edition January 1998
336 pages, ISBN 1-56592-347-2

This second edition covers all of the features of bash Version 2.0, while still applying to bash Version 1.x. It includes one-dimensional arrays, parameter expansion, more pattern-matching operations, new commands, security improvements, additions to ReadLine, improved configuration and installation, and an additional programming aid, the bash shell debugger.

GNU Emacs Pocket Reference

By Debra Cameron
1st Edition November 1998
64 pages, ISBN 1-56592-496-7

O'Reilly's *Learning GNU Emacs* covers the most popular and widespread of the Emacs family of editors. The *GNU Emacs Pocket Reference* is a companion volume to *Learning GNU Emacs*. This small book, covering Emacs version 20, is a handy reference guide to the basic elements of this powerful editor, presenting the Emacs commands in an easy-to-use tabular format.

sed & awk, 2nd Edition

By Dale Dougherty & Arnold Robbins
2nd Edition March 1997
432 pages, ISBN 1-56592-225-5

sed & awk describes two text manipulation programs that are mainstays of the Unix programmer's toolbox. This edition covers the sed and awk programs as they are mandated by the POSIX standard and includes discussion of the GNU versions of these programs.

Effective awk Programming, 3rd Edition

By Arnold Robbins
3rd Edition May 2001
448 pages, ISBN 0-596-00070-7

Effective awk Programming delivers complete coverage of the awk 3.1 language and the most up-to-date coverage of the POSIX standard for awk available anywhere. Author Arnold Robbins clearly distinguishes standard awk features from GNU awk (gawk)–specific features, shines light into many of the "dark corners" of the language and devotes two full chapters to example programs. This book is the official "User's Guide" for the GNU implementation of awk.

O'REILLY®

To order: *800-998-9938* • *order@oreilly.com* • *www.oreilly.com*
Online editions of most O'Reilly titles are available by subscription at *safari.oreilly.com*
Also available at most retail and online bookstores.

sed & awk Pocket Reference, 2nd Edition

By Arnold Robbins
Second Edition June 2002
64 pages, 0-596-00352-8

The *sed & awk Pocket Reference* is a handy, quick reference guide to frequently used functions, commands, and regular expressions used for day-to-day text processing needs. This book is a companion to both *sed & awk*, Second Edition and *Effective awk Programming*, Third Edition.

Evil Geniuses in a Nutshell

By Illiad
1st Edition April 2000
132 pages, ISBN 1-56592-861-X

The follow-up to the highly successful first collection of *User Friendly* comic strips, *Evil Geniuses in a Nutshell* tells the continuing tale of Columbia Internet, "the friendliest, hardest-working and most neurotic little Internet Service Provider in the world." *User Friendly* reads like Dilbert for the Open Source community. It provides outsiders a light-hearted look at the world of the hard core geek and allows those who make their living dwelling in this world a chance to laugh at themselves.

Unix System Administration

Essential System Administration, 3rd Edition

By Æleen Frisch
3rd Edition August 2002
1176 pages, ISBN 0-596-00343-9

This is the definitive practical guide for Unix system administration, covering all the fundamental and essential tasks required to run such divergent Unix systems as Solaris, Linux, AIX, IRIX, BSD and more. Beginners and experienced administrators alike will quickly be able to apply its principles and advice to solve everyday problems.

Essential System Administration Pocket Reference

By Æleen Frisch
1st Edition November 2002
144 pages, ISBN 0-596-00449-4

This pocket reference brings together all the important Unix and Linux system administration information in a single compact volume. Not only are all of the important administrative commands covered, but this reference also includes the locations and formats of important configuration files (including both general system databases like the password and group files as well as the configuration files for major subsystems like DNS, DHCP and sendmail).

Using Samba, 2nd Edition

By Jay Ts, Robert Eckstein &
David Collier-Brown
2nd Edition February 2003
556 pages, ISBN 0-596-00256-4

The second edition of *Using Samba*
thoroughly covers configuration of
the new Samba versions, including
the SWAT graphical configuration
tool. The book also explores Samba's
new role as a secondary domain
controller, its support for the use of
Windows 2000 security on the host
Unix system, and Samba's better
integration with SSL security. Every-
thing is here, from basic installation
and configuration to advanced topics
in security, trouble-shooting, and
special environments.

Unix Power Tools, 3rd Edition

By Shelley Powers, Jerry Peek, Tim
O'Reilly & Mike Loukides
3rd Edition October 2002
1156 pages, ISBN 0-596-00330-7

In addition to vital information on
Linux, Darwin and BSD, *Unix Power
Tools*, 3rd Edition now offers more
coverage of bash, zsh and other new
shells, along with discussions on
modern utilities and applications.
Several sections focus on security
and Internet access, acknowledging
that most Unix boxes are connected
to the Internet. And there is a new
chapter on access to Unix from Windows, addressing the heterogeneous
nature of systems today.

Unix CD Bookshelf, Version 3.0

By O'Reilly & Associates
Version 3.0 Edition January 2003
614 pages, ISBN 0-596-00392-7

Version 3.0 of O'Reilly's *Unix CD
Bookshelf* gives programmers convenient access to their favorite books,
all from their CD-ROM drive. We've
updated this best-selling product
with the electronic versions of 7 of
our most popular Unix books: *Unix
Power Tools*, 3rd Edition, *Learning
the Korn Shell*, 2nd Edition, *Learning
the Unix Operating System*, 5th Edition, *sed & awk*, 2nd Edition, *Learning the vi Editor*, 6th Edition, *Unix in
a Nutshell*, 3rd Edition, and *Mac OS
X for Unix Geeks*. Also included is a
paperback version of *Unix in a
Nutshell*.

System Performance Tuning, 2nd Edition

By Gian-Paolo D. Musumeci &
Mike Loukides
2nd Edition February 2002
336 pages, ISBN 0-596-00284-X

System Performance Tuning covers
two distinct areas: performance tuning, or the art of increasing performance for a specific application, and
capacity planning, or deciding what
hardware best fulfills a given role.
Underpinning both subjects is the
science of computer architecture.
This book focuses on the operating
system, the underlying hardware,
and their interactions. For system
administrators who want a hands-on
introduction to system performance,
this is the book to recommend.

O'REILLY®

To order: *800-998-9938* • *order@oreilly.com* • *www.oreilly.com*
Online editions of most O'Reilly titles are available by subscription at *safari.oreilly.com*
Also available at most retail and online bookstores.

DNS and BIND, 4th Edition

By Paul Albitz & Cricket Liu
4th Edition April 2001
622 pages, ISBN 0-596-00158-4

DNS and BIND, 4th Edition, covers BIND 9, which implements many new and important features, as well as BIND 8, on which most commercial products are based. There's also more extensive coverage of NOTIFY, IPv6 forward and reverse mapping, transaction signatures and the new DNS Security Extensions; and a section on accommodating Windows 2000 clients, servers, and Domain Controllers.

Exim: The Mail Transfer Agent

By Philip Hazel
1st Edition July 2001
632 pages, ISBN 0-596-00098-7

Exim is the default mail transport agent installed on some Linux systems; it runs on many versions of Unix and is suitable for any TCP/IP network with any combination of hosts and end-user mail software. It is open source, scalable, rich in features, and—best of all—easy to configure. This official guide is written by Philip Hazel, the creator of Exim.